THE
HOLE
OF
EVERYTHING,
NEBRASKA

THE
HOLE
OF
EVERYTHING,
NEBRASKA

POEMS BY MAX SEIFERT

Winner of the 2015
Florence Kahn Memorial Award

National Federation of State Poetry Societies
www.nfsps.com

The Hole of Everything, Nebraska
© 2015 by Max Seifert

Published May 2015
The National Federation of State Poetry Societies, Inc.
www.nfsps.com

Editing and design by Kathy Lohrum Cotton

Printed in the United States of America
CreateSpace, Charleston, South Carolina

ISBN-13: 978-1511867900
ISBN-10: 1511867906

For Michael Seifert
1947–2013

CONTENTS

Foreword, ix

From the Judges, xi

Acknowledgments, xiii

Cherry County Highway Sans Terminus, 1

Squaw Voice Hill, The Hole of Everything, Nebraska, #1, 3

Let All Mortal Flesh Keep Silence, 4

The Hole of Everything Tribesmen Little Leaguers, 5

The Embalmer, 7

Squaw Voice Hill, The Hole of Everything, Nebraska, #2, 8

Trends in Population, 9

A Nocturne for Coach in the Hole of Everything, 11

Nebraska, The Hole of Everything, 13

Cherry County Smoking Section, 15

Max Seifert, 17

The Judges, 18

NFSPS College/University Competition, 20

FOREWORD

Max Seifert was a University of Iowa student studying in France his junior year when he submitted a manuscript to the National Federation of State Poetry Societies' first online contest. NFSPS began to receive and process applications and manuscripts through the online manager Submittable.com for the 2015 College/University-Level Poetry Competition.

After months of honing new contest mechanics, the three-member committee, plus our first online-manuscript judges— James F. Ahearn, Jim Barton and Rosemerry Wahtola Trommer—announced two fine young poets as winners. For his manuscript, *The Hole of Everything, Nebraska*, Max Seifert of Wilmette, Illinois, received the generous Florence Kahn Memorial Award.

Seifert describes his collection as "a dream of the American Midwest and its open spaces—its parking lots and cornfields, its baseball diamonds, its slaughterhouses—sites of suffering and gritty miracles. . . .We never lose the sense that we are strangers in this town, tourists to the unmonumental in modern America. These poems lead us 'violently, by our necks, to life.'"

As you read *The Hole of Everything, Nebraska*, we hope you will be challenged by this unique Midwest perspective and enjoy the creative gifts of Max Seifert.

> Chairman Shirley Blackwell, New Mexico
> Chapbook Editor Kathy Cotton, Illinois
> Committee Member Heather Holland, Utah

FROM THE JUDGES

From the combined scores of three independent judges, *The Hole of Everything, Nebraska* was chosen from manuscripts submitted by students across the nation to the 2015 NFSPS College/University-Level Poetry Competition. Each judge made his or her choices for the top six manuscripts, assigning each a score from 1 to 10. Max Seifert's score took the Florence Kahn Memorial Award. Following are excerpts from the judges' comments.

JAMES AHEARN, MICHIGAN

I found the manuscript to be the most memorable of all those submitted by virtue of its title. The title word *Hole* moved in my mind from *hole* to *whole* and back again throughout the poems: from the name of a creek, a town, a little league baseball team to even the entire state of Nebraska—a unique and ingenious element in the overall manuscript.

JIM BARTON, ARKANSAS

Great use of imagery, sense of place. Well worth reading again and again. Brings place from just a space to the fields of the reader's imagination.

ROSEMERRY WAHTOLA TROMMER, COLORADO

Each poem stands alone, but as a collection, it adds up to more than the sum of its parts. Muscular language carries these poems. The images are equal parts terrific and terrible—for instance the cow tongues "stretching through the holes in the shock fence." A collection full of paradox, mystery, what is unsaid and what must be said.

ACKNOWLEDGMENTS

David Freeman was the first person to read every one of the poems in this chapbook. He met me at Prairie Lights Bookstore every Friday at 4:00 and helped me believe that it was worth writing. Conversations with Lila Cutter and Kelvin Ang Teck Jiang on early drafts completely changed the face of the project.

I'm grateful to my amazing poet-teachers at the University of Iowa: Justin Jannise, for going around the whole/hole ellipse with me so many times, and Robyn Schiff for making me read *Sun Under Wood* and for articulating things that I did not know that I knew. Billy Lantta was, and will forever be, my go-to sci-fi expert; if this chapbook had a soundtrack it'd be compiled by Benji Goldsmith. Adam Jaschen respected Noble Silence with me, and any imaginative thought I have can be traced back to summers in Conner Russell's backyard. Ike Lang dealt with all my insecurities. Kathy Cotton was an incredible designer to work with and was the Weight Watchers coach for this chapbook's significant slimming down. I'm still writing poems to try to impress Molly English.

Special thanks to my father, Hank Seifert, for reading me four out of the seven Harry Potter novels and to Vicki for being a wonderful stepmother and a very timely notary. My uncle, for whom *The Hole of Everything*, is dedicated, is an inspiration for every poem I write and every day that I live.

–Max Seifert

CHERRY COUNTY HIGHWAY SANS TERMINUS

Gaining speed now: the bird flies
past my windshield before I can gauge
its species, its call dying somewhere

in my wake—
it's like being fourteen,
a tabby cat licking its coat clean of lint &,

turning to the paws, finding no lint, but blood
instead, around the follicles where the lint
should have been, tripping mushrooms

in the backseat of a Jeep Wrangler—it's easy going
for me here, but I won't let you make the same
mistake: the highway is a thick coffin (the poet

that lives below me writes daily aubades
for each American highway; it's a rotten idea),
for roadkilt elk carcasses all wrought grotesquely

like eunuchs pinned to the spruces that grow
at the treeline as warnings for the cliff face,
or the fleshy spermatozoa of mouse

intestines that the tabby cat has left flush on
the stoop. I'm serious when I promise endlessness
& I'm always promising: I promise flesh, I promise

to not rot by the roadside, I promise spruce tree
air fresheners hung from the rearview, arias
in castrato from the radio. I promised you

I'd slip into the Nebraska night & not return
without something still breathing beneath
my canines, I promised myself I'd face the cliff

& come sliding to its edge—my tires making smoke
of sand—clawing the steering wheel while my teeth
saw into my teeth, my tongue without clean exit.

SQUAW VOICE HILL, THE HOLE
OF EVERYTHING, NEBRASKA, #1

Once, the Natives
found a creek, cold &
clear, smack in the middle
of a thick field of tallgrass.
They named it Hole of Everything
in their Native tongue, but didn't survive
long enough to explain just what they meant.

LET ALL MORTAL FLESH KEEP SILENCE

Her mother dies & she lies down
on the hardwood floor. She learns

how to play baseball catch & the rule of thirds.
She believes in God & then she doesn't,

but she keeps the songs close to her tongue
as she makes wide, slow circles

on her seven-speed underneath the neon
in the Hy-Vee parking lot. Are you paying

attention? she asks her father & the girls
from school. The pedals are digging into

her bare feet as she climbs up Squaw Voice Hill
& rides past the cemetery, the old gears moaning

while the sun is still distant, pale & blue.
Today, she is writing new hymns

for the rusting fire hydrants, the fresh black hairs
grown on her forearm, & the sleeping dogs

leashed to tetherball poles At the slaughterhouse
she exhales slowly. Any moment now,

the cows will come
bumbling over to lick the dewy sweat

from between her fingers, their tongues barely
fitting through the holes in the shock fence.

THE HOLE OF EVERYTHING
TRIBESMEN LITTLE LEAGUERS

The cheerleaders go
silent & chain-smoke
in foul territory.

Like death by lightning strike:
the shortstop caught looking,
the center fielder swinging.

Inning after inning,
the third baseman & catcher
flailing like wrung chickens.

The opposing catcher's mitt
hand goes numb with the smack
of leather against leather.

Game after game,
twenty-seven straight—
a season of strikeouts.

The Team Moms jerry-rig
a bake sale to buy more
zeros for the analog scoreboard.

The third base coach's hand
signals become increasingly abstract,
verge on meaninglessness.

When will they spit out their Bazooka
gum? When will they walk, at once,
into the outfield floodlights?

The Hole of Everything
is rooting for the home team,
& they won't ever win.

THE EMBALMER

They come to him in all states of disarray, all
of them, it seems, these days, eviscerated
or else torn shells, victims to an ugly something
that sat still for years on end.

The embalmer is very talented. They ask him
for advice: there is an in-law's Rosh Hashanah
dinner in Philadelphia & then a present
for a Bar Mitzvah & does he sing
when he prays & could they hear
just one beautifully aspirated *h*—

A check will be fine,
yes, & a merlot lipstick will hide the blue
in their Cupid's bows, & a shofar can be fashioned
from even a small goat's horn, & tufts of hair
can be plucked from underneath their fingernails
with tweezers, & sutures sown into the mandible
will keep it closed. No, he says,
he repeats only a few short words in the shower
at night with the lights turned off, smelling
the formaldehyde lift from his skin in the steam.

All of the glass in the funeral home is stained
       to resemble prairie flowers.

SQUAW VOICE HILL, THE HOLE
OF EVERYTHING, NEBRASKA, #2

Legislature has tried changing the name twice:
once to Springfield—in 1972—and once
to The-Air-a-Stallion-Might-Know-at-Full-Gallop.

TRENDS IN POPULATION

They're pulling into their garages
& promptly cutting their
engines. They're flocking
to exceptionally high places
to admire the view.

Plug-in appliances are staying
in the kitchen. The train conductor
has stopped hovering over
his emergency brake.

Stretching taut thick ropes, they're
tying sophisticated knots to hang-dry
their laundry & secure
their truck hitches.

Each day in H.O.E. births
new mothers & grandmothers.
New half-, step-, & godmothers.

There are new aunts & uncles,
cousins of varying orders
of removal, throngs of babysitters
& dogsitters, a new legion
of landscapers & mailmen.

The suicide rate, of late, is dropping down,
diving faster than anyone can see. All

around H.O.E., family trees are drooping
low, slumped with the weight
of full & plump fruit.
Some heavy magic has settled
into the Hole of Everything &
it's dragging us violently,
by our necks, to life.

A NOCTURNE FOR COACH
IN THE HOLE OF EVERYTHING

Living in Baltimore, alone
& very poor, working nights, hard boiling
six eggs in the morning before bed, driving
the thirty-eight bus from Sparrows Point,
never far from the radio playing
the late-night reruns of Orioles' games
& country rock. There were moments,
in the dark of his apartment, where he'd try hard
to recall the last time he'd spoken to anyone.

It had stopped raining not long
before the old factory collapsed. The two o'clock
westbound thirty-eight was empty that night.
Half-asleep, he first saw the concrete dust
gently nudging the bus's sides
& thought how strange things had gotten of late
when an iron stanchion came crashing through
a streetlight. Inside the thick-glassed bus,
he heard only the dreamy hum of the engine
as it rolled through the thickening cloud.
The buttresses torn jagged from their frames,
the shards of glass
already settling into a thick loam,
the small things crushed, completely—
he willed the machine's steady glide.

Long after practice is over, he stoops
low to the flatness of the field.
He closes his eyes & drives the route—
the whole route, Sparrows Point
to Fort Howard—again.
He opens his eyes, he cannot think of his wife.

NEBRASKA, THE HOLE OF EVERYTHING

I'm pulled back to Nebraska
again, where all I can think to do is lie

down on the gravel parking lot
& listen. The Hole of Everything closes up

shop early. They flip off the light & leave
their doors unlocked. I need a Nebraska

with storm doors that haven't quite come
loose from their hinges. The dogs have nothing

to bark at, here. The few streetlights burnt
out three decades ago & the moon tucks

itself into the gaps in the spine
of Nebraska. Looking back

on town from one of its sleep-stretched
limbs, there's no telling corn field

from town hall from cemetery from black baseball
diamond—I'm back in Nebraska & I've started

drinking moonshine in my motel room. Not bothering
with the bedside lamp. At night, it's easy,

believing there's really nothing where you thought
the schoolyard, & the war memorial, & the fire

station might be. Somewhere far off,
there's the sound of the slaughterhouse dragging

its ceaseless weight. In June, my father will turn
sixty. Nebraska, I'm looking for the shallow ocean

that you used to be: boot-high saltwater & blue
in every direction.

CHERRY COUNTY SMOKING SECTION

It's funny—
the world being

boundless & ever-expanding—that
you should happen

upon our little
saltbox bar in our

nothing town
& that you would

look so very familiar
to so many of us, & seem

to naturally speak
with our very particular tongue.

MAX SEIFERT

Max Seifert of Wilmette, Illinois, is a creative writing student at the University of Iowa, where he edits poetry for *earthwords: the undergraduate review* and interns with the International Writing Program. His work has previously appeared in *Ink Lit Mag* and *plain china: national anthology of undergraduate writing*. His improv troupe, Skinny Horses, and punk band, Riot Fire, are regulars in the Iowa City basement-show scene. This chapbook is the product of tireless support from his friends and family and the University of Iowa creative writing staff.

THE JUDGES

JAMES F. AHEARN, a perennial prizewinner at the NFSPS Annual Poetry Contest awards, has consistently placed in the top ten in multiple categories for more than a decade. His poems have appeared regularly in *Encore* and anthologies published by the Poetry Society of Michigan (PSM). Ahearn coauthored with Joye Giroux *A Reintroduction to Poetry: A Poet's Workshop Experiences and Tips* (2009) and also published essays and poetry in *Boundary Waters Journal*. He has served PSM as vice president for four years, president from 2010 to 2013, and annual contest coordinator since 2009. He lives in Rochester, Michigan, where he conducts a monthly poetry group.

JIM BARTON serves as first vice president and membership chair for NFSPS and treasurer of both the Poets' Roundtable of Arkansas and his local branch. He has four collections of poetry, including the Morris Chapbook Award winner, *At the Bird Museum*. He has won awards nationwide and his poetry has been published in such venues as *The Lyric, The Mid-America Poetry Review, Louisiana Literature* and *The Mississippi Review*. He is a convention and seminar speaker throughout the South and a national and regional poetry judge. Barton believes that a world without poetry is a world without light and that the future of poetry is bright indeed.

ROSEMERRY WAHTOLA TROMMER lives in southwest Colorado. Her poetry has appeared in *O Magazine*, on *A Prairie Home Companion*, in back alleys and on river rocks. Her poetry collections include *The Less I Hold, The Miracle Already Happening: Everyday Life with Rumi, Intimate Landscape* and

Holding Three Things at Once (Colorado Book Award finalist). She served as San Miguel County's first poet laureate and directed the Telluride Writers Guild for ten years. Trommer travels widely to perform poetry and music and to teach and, since 2004, has maintained a poem-a-day practice. Visit her at www.wordwoman.com.

A seven-member planning committee for a National Federation of State Poetry Societies college-level scholarship met on June 26, 1988, at the NFSPS convention in Salt Lake City, Utah. The committee included:

Susan Steven Chambers, Good Thunder, MN
Robert E. DeWitt, Green Cove Springs, FL
Melba C. Dungey, Morgantown, WV
Max Golightly, Provo, UT
Ralph Hammond, Arab, AL
Edna Meudt, Dodgeville, WI
Golda Foster Walker, Baton Rouge, LA

The scholarship was subsequently named in loving memory of Edna Meudt, who died in April 1989. Meudt was a charter member and past president of NFSPS and a member of the Wisconsin Fellowship of Poets. Her wisdom and staunch support helped to make the dream of this award a reality.

In 1999, Florence Kahn, a long-time member of the Miami-Earth Chapter of the Florida State Poets Association, made a generous bequest to the NFSPS scholarship fund. At the 1999 convention in Atlanta, Georgia, the name of the award was changed to the NFSPS Scholarship Award, with one manuscript chosen for the Edna Meudt Memorial Award and one for the Florence Kahn Memorial Award.

At the 2001 convention in Melbourne, Florida, the name of the award was changed to the NFSPS College/University-Level Poetry Competition. It was open to juniors and seniors at accredited colleges and universities. At the 2003 convention in Sioux Falls, South Dakota, the competition was opened to freshmen and sophomores as well.

For the 2015 competitions, manuscripts were accepted and judged online for the first time, utilizing the submission manager, Submittable.com. Also a first for the 2015 contests was the publication and marketing of the chapbooks as perfect-bound paperbacks. The committee included Shirley Blackwell of New Mexico, Kathy Cotton of Illinois, and Heather Holland of Utah.

Annual contest guidelines are posted on the NFSPS website, www.nfsps.com.

Made in the USA
Lexington, KY
24 June 2015